D0717605

YOGA DOGS™

RR
RAVETTE PUBLISHING

First published by Ravette Publishing 2011

Ravette Publishing Limited
PO Box 876
Horsham
West Sussex RH12 9GH

ISBN: 978-1-84161-357-4

On your marks ... get set ...

BOBBY

Rock 'n' roll baby

LILLY

Full Boat Pose
(Paripurna Navasana)

I'm in a league
of my own

ROMEO

Tree Pose

(Vrksasana)

I ain't nothing but a Hound Dog!

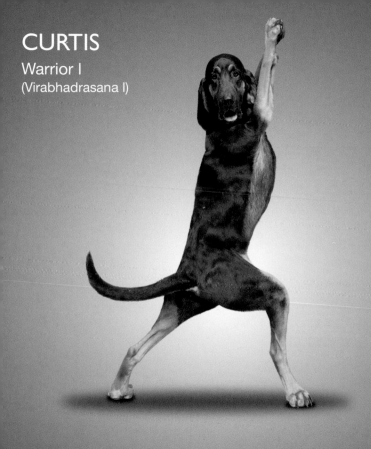

CURTIS

Warrior I
(Virabhadrasana I)

Who says you can't teach an old dog new tricks?

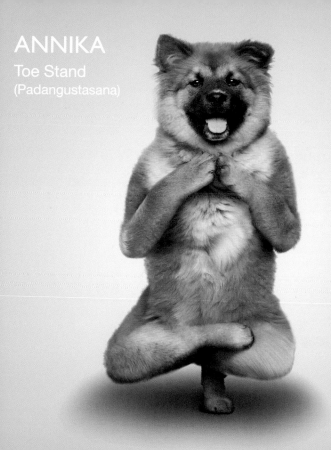

ANNIKA

Toe Stand

(Padangustasana)

How do I

get out

of this?

TINY
Kukkutasana
(Rooster Pose)

I'm all

ears!

MATISSE

Upward Facing Dog
(Urdhva Mukha Svanasana)

Whoops!!
Not quite what
I had in mind

ARIES

Wide Angle Seated Forward Bend
(Upavistha Konasana)

It really is
this big!

DUKE
Warrior II
(Virabhadrasana II)

Sit and stay
in the
moment

CAESAR

Bound Angle Pose

(Baddha Konasana)

I'm not

listening

to you

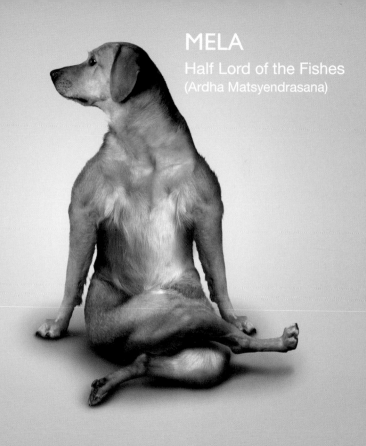

MELA

Half Lord of the Fishes
(Ardha Matsyendrasana)

Reach

for the

Stars!

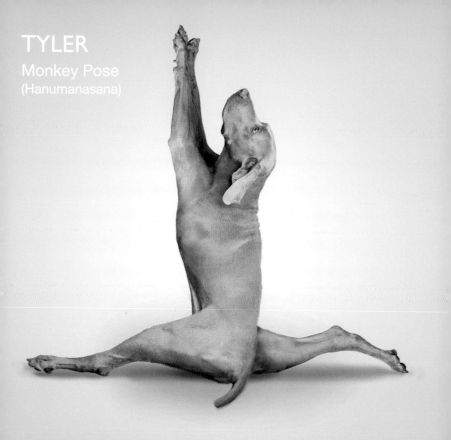

TYLER
Monkey Pose
(Hanumanasana)

There's more
to life than
being cute

LOLA

One Arm Handstand
(Eka Hasta Adho Mukha Vrksasana)

Let your paws
lead the way

NANUK
Warrior III
(Virabhadrasana III)

Hey ... things
are looking up!

TAZ
Plow Pose
(Halasana)

Can I have my treat now?

SUKI
Triangle Pose
(Trikonasana)

Man's best

flexible

friend

MELA

Scorpion Pose

(Vrischikasana)

We all have our hang-ups!

CONTE
Firefly Pose
(Tittibhasana)

A round

of

applaws

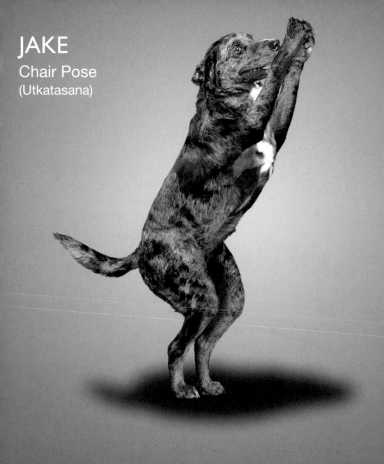

JAKE
Chair Pose
(Utkatasana)

Other titles available in this series ...

	ISBN	Price
Yoga Cats - The Purrfect Workout	978-1-84161-356-7	£4.99

How to order   Please send a cheque/postal order in £ sterling, made payable to 'Ravette Publishing' for the cover price of books and allow the following for post & packaging ...

UK & BFPO	70p for the first book & 40p per book thereafter
Europe and Eire	£1.30 for the first book & 70p per book thereafter
Rest of the world	£2.20 for the first book & £1.10 per book thereafter

RAVETTE PUBLISHING LTD
PO Box 876, Horsham, West Sussex RH12 9GH
Tel: 01403 711443   Fax: 01403 711554   Email: ravettepub@aol.com

Prices and availability are subject to change without prior notice.